Living with ADD

When You're Not The One Who Has It

A Self-Care Workbook for Partners

Mimi Handlin, MSW

Wasteland Press
Shelbyville, KY USA
www.wastelandpress.net

Living With ADD When You're Not The One Who Has It
A Self-Care Workbook For Partners
by Mimi Handlin, MSW

First Printing – September 2005
ISBN: 1-933265-77-9

Printed in the U.S.A.

Author's Note

This publication is designed to provide helpful and informative material on the subject matter covered. It is sold with the understanding that the author is not engaged in providing legal, financial, medical, psychological, or any other professional services. If expert assistance or counseling is needed, the services of a competent professional should be sought. The worksheets in this book are not intended to be a substitute for psychotherapy.

TABLE OF CONTENTS

INTRODUCTION

- She's always late. I can never depend on her to show up on time.

- He'll say, "You never told me that!" when I know I did.

- Our yard looks like a garbage dump from all the stuff he brings home. I'm embarrassed to ask anyone over.

- She interrupts me constantly when I'm talking, without an apology or an "Excuse me."

- It takes him two weeks to mow the lawn. And that's after I've reminded him ten times to finish it.

- She's spent a fortune on filing and organizing systems, but her papers are still piled up to the ceiling. I don't go into our office anymore.

- She blew up at me out of the blue and said horrible things. Twenty minutes later, she acted as if nothing happened.

- He hasn't been able to keep a job for more than six months. Whenever he quits, it's always somebody else's fault.

- She charges things online without worrying about how we're going to pay for them. Our credit cards are all maxed out.

Do any of the above complaints ring a bell? If your partner has attention deficit disorder, you may be wondering: *is this book about us?* Although every relationship is different, loving someone with ADD can be quite challenging. In response to their behaviors, our feelings may vary from slight irritation to overwhelming frustration, hurt, stress, and anger. This is not to say that all ADD marriages are unhappy. Most people with ADD have wonderful characteristics, such as spontaneity, directness, creativity, charisma, and unlimited energy. In many relationships, those positive traits exceed the problems. For others, the difficult symptoms of the disorder, such as disorganization, broken promises, outbursts of anger, and impulsivity outweigh the positives, and the situation is unbearable—especially if the person with ADD isn't getting treatment and support.

This workbook is different from other books about attention deficit disorder, because it was written from the perspective of a non-ADD partner. These pages don't focus on taking care of your ADD spouse or making your relationship work. They are about taking care of yourself. Consequently, as you become healthier and happier, your partner may reap the benefits and your relationship could get better.

The main message of this book is that sometimes it's OK and even imperative to put yourself first. (Or at least second, if you have kids!) Living with and loving a partner with ADD can be tough at times, and you deserve special care and support. This book is for you.

ABOUT THIS BOOK

First, some important clarifications: Although ADD affects both men and women, I've used the pronoun "he" for consistency and because it was more natural for me. If you have a female partner, this book is also for you——the issues will be just as relevant. Think "she" instead.

The abbreviations for attention deficit disorder have been changed throughout the years. Although professionals most commonly use ADHD, I have chosen ADD for this book because it is most familiar to the public.

And finally, the jokes about ADD were not intended to be offensive, only to lighten up an often-difficult situation.

- **Chapter 1** is for folks who *think* their partners may have attention deficit disorder. If your partner has already been diagnosed, you may want to skip this chapter, review it, or browse through "*Resources for Learning.*"

- **Chapter 2** offers insights into frustrations you may be feeling when your partner is in denial, or when the medication isn't helping enough. Whether your spouse has received a diagnosis or is resisting one, you will no doubt relate to something here.

- **Chapter 3** is about validating your experiences with a partner who has ADD. When you're reeling from his hurtful words or he denies his behavior, you can end up blaming yourself or doubting your own reality.

- **Chapter 4** helps you understand yourself better as an individual and as a partner. The goal is to eventually allow you more choice when responding to your spouse's behaviors. If you aren't yet aware of alternatives, you may be parenting an adult or getting stomach-aches from resentment.

- **Chapter 5** is designed to turn new or old insights about problems in your relationship into practical solutions. But first, how do you get him to listen?

- **Chapter 6** gets to the bottom line. What attitudes and skills are essential to surviving in an ADD relationship? What's left to try when you are at the end of your rope?

- **Chapter 7** moves beyond surviving into thriving. It's a gift just for you, with ideas and practices to bring you peace.

The worksheets in chapters 3 and 4 are intended to promote awareness. The forms in chapters 5, 6, and 7 are designed to help you resolve difficulties, and build new skills and practices. Some of them may be filled out and kept in the book. Others will be most helpful if they are copied, filled out and placed around your house. Feel free to look at those pages as templates to give you ideas or help you get started. Change or add to them so they feel right for you.

MY STORY

I met my husband in 1980. He was compassionate, intense, and the most interesting man I'd every known. He was driven by an energy that wouldn't allow him to sit still for a minute without talking, humming, or bobbing a leg. On vacations, lying on a beach was intolerable for him. His idea of rest was to keep moving and exploring until he dropped. Although he read articles voraciously and could brilliantly discuss any issue, I never saw him read a book. His bright, creative side was often overshadowed by a quick anger and simmering frustration that was mysterious even to him. As a way to channel the anger into something positive, he became a fearless union organizer and a passionate advocate for the less fortunate. He even practiced tai chi and aikido for the same reason, but the anger remained, unfettered and always present.

One of his most striking characteristics was that he rarely made eye contact. His head was constantly turning in response to what was going on around him. He was in a constant state of creativity, building ideas, concepts, and plans that never quite made it to fruition. This played out in projects such as our huge, old house, which was always under construction. His goal was to finish it from the top down, but he never got below the attic.

Although these characteristics had positive aspects, they made for a difficult marriage. I wasn't demanding, but it was hard to hang pictures on two-by-fours. Before we had kids, I made him install a heating system that would melt the icicles inside the windows. Any intimacy between us lacked depth because he was so easily distracted. My romantic rivals were random, exciting thoughts or sounds outside the window. Usually, when we were the closest, it was after we resolved a conflict that he had instigated.

Often his anger didn't make sense to me or seemed way out of proportion to the event that triggered it. I walked on eggshells and lived in a state of caution, hurt, and confusion. During so much of the marriage, I was exhausted from our emotionally laden late-night talks and his second winds. If we weren't discussing why he was upset, he wanted my companionship while he sorted through jumbles of disorganized paperwork after eleven at night. He didn't want me to do anything—just sit beside him for support. I just wanted to go to bed.

My husband was a good person and he tried hard to get beyond the chaos. That's why I loved him. And that's also why he saw a string of therapists who helped him create all sorts of explanations for his inner turmoil. But none felt true. We spent hours in marriage counseling, ending up with better communication skills, but no real insights into why our marriage was so hard.

In 1986, he was diagnosed with acute leukemia. For over two years, all of that unfocused energy was directed towards surviving chemotherapy and a bone marrow transplant. There was no time for conflict, only for a love between us that was uncomplicated by blame, frustration, and distractions. He died in 1989, leaving me with three small children and many unresolved feelings about the difficulties in our marriage.

During the ensuing years, our son was diagnosed with attention deficit disorder. I didn't link it to his dad's behavior, because it manifested in such a different way, and I wasn't aware of the genetic component. I also thought it occurred only in children. Then I started a business with a warm, gregarious woman who was a lot like my late husband. She was also on medication for ADD. The feelings stirred up in me by her inability to listen, focus, or take responsibility for her own frustrations were strikingly familiar. So was sitting beside her while she sorted through mountains of paperwork. That partnership taught me about ADD and lit the way to the past. Her struggles and dysfunctions were a reflection of my husband's, and I finally knew that he had a brain disorder. He did love me and his frustrations were not my fault—or his. Fifteen years after his death, I understood.

Since that time, my memories of my husband include a loss for what could have been, if only we had known about the ADD. I wrote this book because I wish I had possessed such a resource when I was married. My purpose was not only to help other struggling spouses and partners, but, retrospectively, to heal myself.

Prelude

*"Keep your eyes open before marriage;
half shut afterwards."*

Benjamin Franklin

YOU LOCKED YOURSELF OUT AGAIN?
A MEDICAL EXPLANATION

Why can't he just listen? How can he lose two appointment books in a month? Why is it so hard for him to complete a chore that takes me ten minutes? If your partner has ADD, you're probably confounded by his thoughts and behaviors.

The most valuable self-care strategy you can utilize is to learn as much as possible about ADD. And the most important fact to know about ADD is that symptoms—such as losing appointment books or being unable to finish the dishes in less than three days—are the result of a real medical condition. It's not something your partner is doing on purpose. Because many of us don't know the biology behind the behaviors that can drive us nuts, we carry unrealistic expectations. We think: "Why can't he just get it together?"

Although there are many theories about the causes of ADD, most professionals agree that it tends to run in families, and it is the result of a neurochemical imbalance that affects the brain. The nervous system produces chemical substances called neurotransmitters that carry information from one nerve cell to another. The neurotransmitters believed to be most strongly involved with ADD are norepinephrine and dopamine. When someone exhibits the symptoms of ADD, their neurotransmitters are not flowing properly.

The part of the brain affected in attention deficit disorder is the prefrontal cortex, which is particularly involved in attention, problem solving, and memory. When the information system isn't working optimally in this part of the brain, people lose their ability to clearly understand and process information. This translates into all of the symptoms we recognize as ADD, including poor decision making, misinterpretation of interpersonal cues, impulsivity, inability to focus, and poor memory.

When your patience bin is empty because your husband locked the keys in his car *again* or forgot why he went to the store, knowing there is a medical reason for his symptoms may calm you down inside.

CHAPTER ONE

I Think He Has It

(FOR THOSE WITH UNDIAGNOSED PARTNERS)

"Whatever advice you give, be short."

Horace

APPROACHING THE SUBJECT

If you suspect your spouse has attention deficit disorder, the next pages are about how to discuss the subject and convince him to get help. Encouraging your partner to acknowledge possible ADD is a huge step towards taking care of yourself. It's often hard to live with someone who has ADD. It's even harder to live with someone who is undiagnosed and untreated.

If you believe your partner has ADD, start a conversation about it. Make sure it's quiet at home and you have a good chance of keeping his attention. Maybe it's easiest to talk with him after the kids are in bed, or across the breakfast table. Just be sure it's not when you're upset or frustrated. It will be hard enough for your spouse to be open to the idea that he may have a disorder, without you coming across as angry or blaming. Reassure your partner that you love him and want to stay in the relationship. When you talk about the possibility of ADD, be sure to emphasize that it's a no-fault disorder such as diabetes or nearsightedness. And let him know that it can be treated, just like diabetes is treated with insulin, and nearsightedness with glasses. The most hopeful fact to tell him is that with proper diagnosis, medication, and other interventions, life *will* get easier.

ONLINE CHECKLISTS
AND QUESTIONNAIRES

Describe the ADD-like traits you've observed in your spouse, and ask if he would be willing to take a few tests home—just out of curiosity. Dr. Daniel Amen offers an adult symptoms checklist on his Website,
www.amenclinics.com

Click on Amen Clinics. Once you're there, you'll find "Online Self-Tests" under the title. These comprehensive, interactive self-tests are scored by the computer.

You can also visit Dr. Ned Hallowell's Website,
www.drhallowell.com

Click on the blue "Resources" tab to access his "Suggested Diagnostic Criteria for Attention Deficit Disorder in Adults."

All of these questionnaires and checklists are not intended for self-diagnosis, but rather as tools to help suggest the possibility of attention deficit disorder. It would be useful for both you and your partner to take the tests. Answer the questions or check off the symptoms based on your observations, and compare answers.

If your partner isn't willing to look at anything, fill one out on your own. Then show him your scores. Another tactic is to ask friends or relatives who know him well to also complete a checklist. Seeing the results from more than "just you" might motivate him to visit a professional.

HOW TO GET HELP

If your partner agrees to be clinically tested, you can take a deep breath. Nothing is going to change today, but at least you're on the right road. In general, the following professionals are licensed or certified to make a diagnosis of ADD: psychologists, medical doctors, neuropsychologists, and psychiatrists. Ideally, the professional you choose should have specific training and experience diagnosing and treating ADD. If you live in a small town, it's probably worth a drive to the nearest teaching hospital to find someone qualified who warrants your confidence.

Good referral sources include the CHADD (Children and Adults with Attention-Deficit/Hyperactivity Disorder) group in your area, other adult ADD support groups, physician and psychologist referral sources, and the *National ADD Directory* (www.ADDresources.org). You can do a search at www.google.com for "ADHD" (your state) and "ADHD" (largest city next to you.)

Cynthia Hammer, MSW, of ADD Resources, has compiled a list of ten questions to ask when looking for an ADD professional.

1. Do you diagnose ADHD? Do you accept my insurance?

2. How long have you been diagnosing this disorder in adults?

3. How many ADHD adults have you diagnosed in the past five years? What percentage of your practice has a primary diagnosis of ADHD?

4. How familiar are you with the day-to-day tribulations of having ADHD? (You're trying to learn if they or someone they are close to has this condition. How intimate is their understanding of ADHD on a daily basis?)

5. What is your treatment philosophy? (Will the clinician work with you and be open to suggestions or will he/she call all the shots? Is their treatment of ADHD the same for everyone or is it individually tailored?)

6. In a subtle way, learn what they do to keep current in their knowledge about adult ADHD and its treatment protocols.

7. How do you make a diagnosis? How many visits will it take and how much will it cost?

8. How long will I have to wait for an appointment?

9. Ask psychologists how they handle the medication part of treatment as psychologists do not have prescriptive authority.

10. Ask physicians (and other medical personnel with prescriptive authority) what medicines they use to treat ADHD.

Keep track of with whom you spoke and how they answered these questions.

WHAT TO EXPECT

ADD is not diagnosed by one medical or genetic test. It's a careful process involving family histories, ADD symptom checklists, standardized behavior rating scales, and multiple interviews with clients and others who know the patient well. Clinical guidelines that doctors or mental health professionals use for a diagnosis are provided in a book called the *Diagnostic and Statistical Manual of Mental Disorders, Fourth Edition, Text Revision*. It's often referred to simply as the DSM-IV.

Because everyone experiences ADD symptoms some of the time, the DSM-IV contains very specific guidelines for determining when the behaviors indicate ADD. Symptoms must appear by the age of seven and continue for at least six months. The most important determinant in adults is that the behaviors or thoughts create a real hardship in at least two areas of a person's life—school, work, home, or social settings. Some questions that may be asked during the interview are:

1. Are the symptoms excessive, long-term, or pervasive? Do you experience them more often than other people your age?

2. Are they a continuous problem as opposed to a reaction to a particular situation?

3. Do the problems occur in several settings or only in one place?

4. When did the problems begin?

5. How seriously are the ADD thoughts and behaviors impacting your life?

6. Are there other related problems or conditions?

The last question is an important one because there are other medical conditions that look like ADD, such as anxiety, depression, thyroid disease, hormone imbalances, and certain mental illnesses. Also, many people diagnosed with ADD have co-existing conditions. These include substance abuse, bipolar disease, learning disabilities, depression, and even sleep apnea.

Your diagnostician should be someone qualified to rule out conditions that mimic ADD and, if there are co-existing conditions, determine which should be dealt with first.

RESOURCES FOR LEARNING

Websites, books, and even videos abound for those interested in learning about adult ADD. Here are some of the most helpful:

WEBSITES:

www.ADDresources.org

Attention Deficit Disorder Resources is a non-profit organization dedicated to helping people with ADD/ADHD achieve their full potential. They provide information, activities, conferences, and membership benefits. They also offer a large lending library of books, audiotapes, and videotapes about ADD.

www.CHADD.org

Children and Adults with Attention-Deficit/Hyperactivity Disorder is a non-profit organization with over 20,000 members and 2,000 affiliates nationwide. They sponsor local support groups, publish a magazine, and provide science-based information to parents, educators, professionals, the media, and the general public.

www.ADDforums.com

ADD Forums is an online community of individuals touched by ADD/ADHD. You can find support, perspective, and information here, as well as good old-fashioned advice from others who share your experiences.

www.ADDvance.com

Kathleen Nadeau, Ph.D. and Patricia Quinn, M.D. (both are internationally recognized authors and authorities on ADD/ADHD) have designed a site to provide answers to questions about ADD for families and individuals at every stage of life, from preschool through retirement years.

www.ADD.org

The Attention Deficit Disorder Association has been an international non-profit organization since 1989. Their mission is to provide information, resources, and networking to adults with ADD/ADHD and to the professionals who work with them.

BOOKS:

Adventures in Fast Forward: Life, Love, and Work for the ADD Adult
by Kathleen Nadeau, Ph.D.

You Mean I'm not Lazy, Stupid or Crazy?! A Self-help Book for Adults with Attention Deficit Disorder
by Kate Kelly, and Peggy Ramundo

Women with Attention Deficit Disorder: Embracing Disorganization at Home and in the Workplace
by Sari Solden

Delivered from Distraction: Getting the Most out of Life with Attention Deficit Disorder
by Edward M. Hallowell and John J. Ratey

ADD Success Stories: A Guide to Fulfillment for Families with Attention Deficit Disorder
by Thom Hartmann

Healing ADD: The Breakthrough Program that Allows You to See and Heal the 6 Types of ADD
by Daniel G. Amen, M.D.

What Does Everybody Else Know That I Don't? Social Skills Help for Adults with Attention Deficit/Hyperactivity Disorder
by Michele Novotni and Randy Petersen

NOTES TO MYSELF

CHAPTER TWO

Issues Around The Diagnosis And Expectations For Change

*"Although the world is full of suffering,
it is full also of the overcoming of it."*

Helen Keller

WHY CAN'T THEY JUST ADMIT IT?

Many of our partners were relieved when they found a reason for their struggles. Yet some of our partners refuse to even consider the possibility of ADD. If you're married to someone in the latter group, you probably feel frustrated and angry. The discovery of adult ADD is a huge "Aha!" moment for us. Finally, it all makes sense. We devour books about ADD, underlining all the phrases that describe our mates. Filled with anticipation of getting help, we eagerly share what we've learned by showing them books, magazine articles, and Internet sites. And our spirits sink when our partners barely glance at them, only to proclaim, "That's not me. I don't have that." Eventually, we find online forums where non-ADD mates can express their frustrations. Or we end up attending ADD support groups alone. Even if every cell of our body knows the partner we love has ADD, convincing him of it can be another story.

Some of our spouses have been willing to look at a few books or take an online test, but that's as far as it has progressed. Others have actually been diagnosed, but won't accept any kind of treatment—at least on a consistent basis. Understanding why it's so difficult to accept an ADD diagnosis may help you find a little objectivity and diffuse your frustration a bit. Here are some reasons:

- If your partner is like everyone else on the planet, he doesn't want to admit something could be "wrong" with him— especially with his brain. It's a particularly painful admission for those who see themselves as strong and competent.

- Many people with ADD are understandably defensive from years of feeling ashamed of their symptoms. By the time they reach adulthood, they've been just plain battered by statements like, "You need to try harder," "Your problem is you don't care," or "It's so easy. Why can't you just do it?"

- No one wants to be different or have special needs. It can be embarrassing and often causes shame.

- Some individuals have a tendency to blame others for their mistakes or shortcomings. Admitting they have ADD implies, even if it wasn't on purpose, that they have played a part in their own problems.

- They may not realize how hurtful or harmful their behavior is to you. An hour after your partner's angry outburst, you're still reeling. He's forgotten all about it.

- One of the symptoms of ADD is inaccurate self-observation. Your partner may not even recognize his struggles, even though you're in a sweat watching him tear through the house every morning searching for his shoes.

- The familiar is always more comfortable. After a lifetime of struggle, it could be scary for your spouse to think that treatment could help him succeed. Would others then expect more from him? What if he couldn't deliver?

- Your spouse may be one of many who don't believe ADD is a real disorder. They think it's an over-diagnosed fad.

ONCE HE'S ON DRUGS,
WILL I FEEL BETTER?

If your partner has just been diagnosed, you may be expecting huge changes with the first dose of medicine. If he's been treated for some time, perhaps you're frustrated because not enough is changing. Although a drug can work wonders to temporarily control impulsivity or reduce distractibility, it can't cure ADD. Along with taking medications, your mate needs to look at overcoming years of detrimental habits, negative thinking, and flawed communication skills. And that's not easy. Most experts agree that healing ADD requires a comprehensive approach. In addition to medication, people can utilize good nutrition, exercise, support, education, coaching, therapy, and relaxation techniques.

One positive aspect of taking medication is that it allows more focus, so your partner will be better able to learn and change—when the desire is there.

If your relationship has become distant and painful, regardless of the medications, a good marriage counselor can help. Don't wait too long. ADD marriages can be full of conflict and tension, especially if your mate has been undiagnosed for a long time. If you choose this route, it's important to find a therapist experienced with ADD relationships. Our issues are unique. In a non-ADD marriage, a person might break an agreement as a subconscious way of expressing anger. A partner with ADD breaks an agreement because he forgot all about it.

NOTES TO MYSELF

CHAPTER THREE

ADD Symptoms And Your Marriage

"Love is a fire. But whether it is going to warm your heart or burn down your house, you can never tell."

Joan Crawford

A TRUE STORY

Susan and Mack love each other deeply, and have been together for fifteen years. They have been stressed by money problems their whole married life, finally culminating in a move to Holland (Mack is a Dutch citizen) so they could receive medical care and welfare. Before they moved, Mack made a minimal income by running a car repair shop in their front yard. Their property was littered with car parts, empty cans of engine oil, and unusable old cars that Mack swore he was going to fix up and sell. Every time Susan looked, there were more junk cars in front of the house. They were growing with the weeds.

Mack liked the problem-solving aspect of being a mechanic, but had difficulty following through with the work. He couldn't maintain a customer base, because it took him too long to finish repairs. Due to the mess in his office, he often lost bills and receipts. They were buried in papers, beer bottles, empty food containers, and tools. Although they were barely making it financially, he managed to buy big-ticket items like a grand piano without budgeting for it. One year, on a whim, they flew to Disneyland. Seeing something he wanted right away provided the motivation Mack needed to fix up and sell a car.

At least once a year, he became excited about some idea for making "big" money. His ideas ranged from building little vacation cabins in the woods behind their house, to creating a recording studio, to installing storage units that the public would rent. All of those ideas had potential, because he was handy and brilliant. Susan would spend hours discussing them with Mack. Then, after a few months, he would lose interest and go on to something else. Every time this happened, Susan felt let down and disappointed.

Mack's back hurt from working on cars and he was often depressed. When Susan came home from work, he was usually in the house, playing the piano or watching TV. He had a quick temper and interpreted any of Susan's concerns about money as excessive worrying or nagging. He didn't seem worried, so she questioned her own reality in spite of monthly trips to the food bank.

Although Susan and Mack had three children, he rarely helped with childcare or housework. As a matter of fact, Susan was afraid to leave him in charge of the kids. He would get lost in an idea or the piano and lose track of them. One day, a neighbor found their four year old daughter meandering on the highway. Susan threatened to leave Mack many times, especially after he blew up at her, lost another customer, or a neighbor made derogatory comments about the junk on their property. She worked three-quarter time, and was almost completely responsible for the kids and the household.

For most of their marriage, Mack had been telling Susan about the wonders of his childhood in Holland and how sure he was of a better life overseas. He would feel less stressed about having to support his family, because the government had a great welfare system. There would be more opportunities for interesting work and maybe he could even make it as a musician. Besides, he wouldn't have to pay three years of back taxes. Sick of holding it all together and because she did love him, Susan decided to give Mack that last chance to improve their lives. They moved to Holland four years ago. When we last spoke, they were barely making it on welfare. He was depressed and spent most of his days sitting around the house playing the piano. Susan was busy learning a new language and culture, going to school, and working in order to support their family.

There is an old saying: "Wherever you go, there you are."

Mack exhibited a number of adult ADD symptoms including:

- *Inability to follow through* when he came up with such great ideas, but lost steam after a while.

- *Distractibility* when he forgot he was watching the kids and let them wander off.

- *Quick temper and defensiveness* when he exploded at Susan for "nagging" him about money.

- *Lack of impulse control* when he saw something he wanted, such as a grand piano or a trip to Disneyland. Never mind that paying for those things took money away from food or the mortgage.

- *Procrastination* when his auto repair work was routine and not as exciting as problem solving.

- *Depression*, either as a comorbid condition or as a result of his life with ADD.

- *Trouble following proper procedures* when he put off filing his taxes for so many years.

- *Poor organization,* as evidenced by his office and property.

THE VALUE OF IDENTIFYING
YOUR PARTNER'S TRAITS

Perhaps if Susan had recognized Mack's behaviors as traits of ADD, their story would have ended differently.

- She would have protected herself from disappointment by refusing to join Mack in his plans for "big money."

- She would have found safer child care, instead of assuming Mack's distractions were an aberration.

- She would have realized her financial concerns were justified, in spite of being called a nag.

- She would have never moved to Holland.

Distancing yourself enough to observe and recognize your partner's specific traits can help you in a number of ways. Documenting them can help you even more. Let's say your partner forgets your birthday most years. Recognizing memory problems as an ADD symptom can protect you from the hurt of believing he does it intentionally. If you know he'll probably forget your birthday next year, you can let go of your pride. Protect your heart by being proactive, and put funny notes around the house about your upcoming day.

It's important to write down the behaviors that are so hard to live with, because seeing them in black and white will help validate your reality. You may stop trusting yourself if your spouse denies what he said or did. If you have something in writing, you can show it to your therapist, support group, and maybe even to your partner if you don't think he will react too defensively. You can keep it as proof of your sanity.

On the next few pages are worksheets to help you document your partner's traits. The first is about his difficult symptoms, and the second is about the other side of the coin. Although ADD symptoms can be hard to deal with, chances are you fell in love with your partner for good reasons. Maybe he can always make you laugh or converse brilliantly about any subject. Documenting your partner's positive traits can help you refresh your love and look at your mate with a new perspective. And if you plan on showing him the first worksheet, you might want to share the second one as well.

ONE SIDE OF THE COIN:
MY PARTNER'S DIFFICULT
ADD BEHAVIORS

1._____
_____
_____
_____
_____
_____
_____
_____
_____
_____
_____
_____
_____

2._____
_____
_____
_____
_____
_____
_____
_____
_____
_____
_____
_____
_____
_____

3._____

_____

_____

_____

_____

_____

_____

_____

4._____

_____

_____

_____

_____

_____

_____

_____

5._____

_____

_____

_____

_____

_____

_____

_____

THE OTHER SIDE OF THE COIN

WHY I LOVE _____ ♥

_____

_____
_____
_____
_____
_____
_____
_____
_____
_____
_____
_____
_____
_____
_____
_____
_____
_____
_____
_____
_____
_____
_____
_____
_____
_____
_____
_____
_____
_____
_____
_____

NOTES TO MYSELF

_____
_____
_____
_____
_____
_____
_____
_____
_____
_____
_____
_____
_____
_____
_____
_____
_____
_____
_____
_____
_____
_____
_____
_____
_____
_____
_____
_____
_____
_____
_____
_____
_____
_____
_____
_____

CHAPTER FOUR

Understanding Ourselves In The Relationship

"I was nauseous and tingly all over.
I was either in love or I had smallpox."

Woody Allen

RECOGNIZING OUR FEELINGS

The difficult traits in our partners can make us feel unloved, irritated, or unbearably stressed. Sometimes, we feel like we've been hit by a train. While we're spinning, it's hard to process exactly what happened. And it can drive us crazy if, a few hours later, our partners act as if nothing occurred. It's not unusual for us to carry around simmering anxiety, anger, or frustration. Or we may feel so exhausted from the conflicts and misunderstandings that we become numb. For the sake of our relationships and our own well-being, it's essential that we make an effort to continually recognize our feelings and the actions that precipitated them. After we tell ourselves the truth, we can tell our partners.

The first step towards becoming clear is to push away any numbness or denial that has developed over the years. If an interaction with our spouse left us feeling uncomfortable in any way, we need to acknowledge it. We may not be able to analyze and understand everything that happened, but we can recognize basic emotions such as hurt or anger. It may only get as far as the thought, "I feel hurt and I don't know why." That's OK. You can figure out why later.

Becoming cognizant of our internal reactions is a skill that takes practice to develop. Our emotions often express themselves in our bodies with signs such as sweaty palms or a racing heart. As we learn to listen to our bodies, we'll be better able to know what we're feeling when our spouses say words or act in ways that upset us. Then we can be clear when we talk about it.

The following are some physical sensations associated with basic emotions.

SENSATIONS OF FEAR

Nausea
Rapid or irregular heart rate

Chest pain
Tightness in stomach and chest
Excessive perspiration
Mouth dryness
Difficulty in breathing
Dizziness

SENSATIONS OF ANGER

Tightness in shoulders and neck
Headache
Nighttime grinding of teeth
Soreness in face from tight jaw
Feeling ready to explode
Trembling or shaking

SENSATIONS OF SADNESS

Heavy, dull feeling in chest
Difficulty waking up and facing the day
Frequent colds and congestion
Loss of appetite
Tired, no energy

WORKSHEET 4A

What do you feel in your body when you are upset with your partner? Is what you experience different or additional to the previous list?

FEAR

_____
_____
_____
_____
_____

ANGER

_____
_____
_____
_____
_____

SADNESS

_____
_____
_____
_____
_____
_____

Sometimes, events with our mates can bring out emotions that have their roots in the past—another relationship, our childhood, etc. *If you find that your body's responses seem out of proportion to what actually happened, it might be helpful to talk things over with a friend, a therapist, or someone else you trust.*

SEPARATING THOUGHTS
FROM FEELINGS

In order to know and tell the truth, it's important to differentiate our thoughts from our feelings. Sometimes we use our thoughts to negate our feelings. For example, let's imagine a woman who is mad because she's been waiting in the rain for her husband who forgot to pick her up. Her feelings are justified, but her thoughts are, "He can't help it. It's not his fault." Or perhaps he's super-defensive so she'll think, "I can't say anything; he'll blow up at me." So she ends up trying to ignore the fact that she's fuming. That doesn't help her or the relationship.

We can also become confused between thoughts and feelings, making it hard to uncover the truth. I knew a woman whose husband had just quit his job. They had two kids and she was terrified. When asked how she felt, she responded, "I feel like he doesn't care about me or the kids. Who is going to pay the bills? I feel like he doesn't think. He just does whatever he wants." That's not expressing how she feels; it's thinking and evaluating her husband's intentions. If she speaks to her husband from that perspective, he'll feel attacked, accused, and will probably stop listening. The real truth is that she was scared. And if he knew that real truth, his response to her might be very different.

How can you learn to separate out your thoughts from your feelings? One way is to notice how many words you are using. A feeling is usually just a few words: "I feel angry." If you go on much more than that, you are probably relating a thought.

Here are examples of words that describe how non-ADD spouses may feel, in alphabetical order: *abandoned, afraid, alone, ambivalent, annoyed, angry, anxious, awed, betrayed, confused, crushed, delighted, diminished, disappointed, embarrassed, enraged, excited, forgiving, frightened, frustrated, glad, grateful, guilty, happy, high, hopeless, hostile, hurt, ignored, impatient, impressed, insane, insecure, irritated, lonely, loving, mean, miserable, overwhelmed, panicked, patient, peaceful, pressured, rejected, relieved, resentful, sad, scared, shocked, threatened, trapped, vulnerable, worried, and wonderful.*

The last two are in reverse alphabetical order, but I wanted to end on a positive note. Take your pick!

The following worksheet is intended to help you become aware of the difference between your thoughts and your feelings. Once you are clear about the distinction, hopefully it will be possible to have more truthful, effective, less accusatory/ defensive conversations with your partner.

WORKSHEET 4B

What happened:

_____

_____

_____

_____

_____

What I thought:

_____

_____

_____

_____

_____

How I felt:

_____

_____

_____

_____

_____

If you can think of more than one incident, take another piece of
paper and keep writing.

WILL THE REAL YOU PLEASE STAND UP?

In our lives, we play many roles—sister, mother, daughter, lover, chauffeur, teacher, and so on. In our ADD marriages, we sometimes take on roles that inaccurately reflect who we are or want to be. This is not our fault. It's the only way we know how to make something happen or to cope with ongoing emotional turmoil.

Non-ADD spouses who find themselves responsible for everything around the house commonly become nags. That seldom works, so we turn into angry witches or . . . what rhymes with witches? When we find ourselves taking care of our mates, we play the role of a mom or a dad. This can become a problem in the bedroom, because no mentally healthy person wants to have sex with a child. When we don't know any other way to respond, we may play the role of the punisher by withdrawing emotionally and physically. Or we become a martyr by holding our hurt inside. Our spouse asks, "What's wrong?" and we reply, "Nothing."

The problem with bottling up our emotions is that eventually we'll act passive-aggressively. Our feelings have to come out somehow. We'll end up slamming doors or aiming little verbal jabs at our partners. Of all these not-so-healthy roles, the one that harms us the most is playing the victim. Then we are stuck, waiting for them to change before we can feel better.

The next worksheet can help you become aware of roles you may be playing in your relationship. Lao Tzu, an ancient Chinese sage, said, "Knowing others is intelligence, knowing yourself is true wisdom."

WORKSHEET 4C

Think about your marriage and any roles you may play (nag, parent, victim, etc.). How do you feel when you find yourself in this position?

_____
_____
_____
_____
_____

What kind of results are you getting?

_____
_____
_____
_____
_____
_____

If you stop what you've been doing, can you think of any healthier ways to get the results you want?

_____
_____
_____
_____
_____
_____
_____

THE RECEIVING END OF THEIR ANGER

As the people closest to our ADD partners, we often get the brunt of their anger. I'm not saying that everyone with ADD takes their frustrations out on their partners, but the problem occurs often enough to warrant some discussion. Misplaced negative emotions come out as sarcasm, and/or anger that are out of proportion to the events that triggered them. They can even enter the realm of verbal abuse.

There are a number of reasons for this distressing side effect of an ADD marriage. Some people with attention deficit disorder tend to seek stimulation in the form of conflict. Others have no impulse control. They just say whatever comes to mind without thinking of how hurtful it is. ADD symptoms can include having a quick trigger point, and small annoyances cause as much anger as huge issues. And a final reason is that stressed partners need to get their anger or frustration out. Unfortunately, we're the nearest targets.

If our partners spew their negative feelings at us often enough, we feel chronically hurt and angry. Or we can get used to it. We don't even notice we've turned into dart boards. The following worksheet can help you recognize your partner's behavior and your internal and external responses. If you are getting the brunt of his anger, chapter 5 offers ideas about how to protect your heart.

WORKSHEET 4D

Are there times when your partner takes his anger or frustration out on you? Keep in mind that sarcasm can be a way of expressing those emotions.

What exactly did he say or do?

_____
_____
_____
_____

How did you feel?

_____
_____
_____
_____

What did you say or do?

_____
_____
_____
_____

Whatever your response, how did you feel later? Did the experience stay with you or were you able to let go of it?

_____
_____
_____
_____

OUR PERSONAL BOUNDARIES

Many non-ADD mates are severely challenged when it comes to developing and keeping boundaries. Boundaries can be described as lines we draw to define all kinds of property. Physical boundaries are easy to see, because they take the form of hedges, doors, electric fences, or even moats with alligators. Emotional boundaries are more intangible, and they are the ones that can cause problems. They define what we are willing to accept, and create the line between *what is me* and what is *someone else.* When our mates have ADD and we find ourselves taking care of them, or feeling invaded by their disorganization and chaos, our boundaries get blurred.

Some of us with fuzzy boundaries don't hold our partners accountable for their actions or choices, because they seem incapable. We may even take over and anticipate their needs when they haven't asked for anything. A problem develops, however, when our spouses give up more and more responsibility as we take more on. We feel manipulated into giving more than we want to and end up angry and resentful.

Although boundary development is an ongoing process, its foundation was built in our childhood. Maybe we were never allowed to say "No" when we were kids. Perhaps our role in the family was to make others happy. If we expressed our own needs or desires, we were given the message that we were bad, selfish people. We carried those feelings with us into adulthood and now we find ourselves with problems saying no or trouble setting limits with our spouses. If we were brought up to believe our role in life is to take care of others, it makes sense that we would choose an ADD mate. Some reasons for blurring of boundaries are fear of:

- Hurting their feelings.

- Making them angry.

- Being seen as selfish or uncaring.

- Being left or abandoned.

- Being punished in some form, such as withdrawal of communication or sex.

- Creating negative consequences for our families: If we don't pay the bills, nobody will.

If you have problems keeping boundaries, the following worksheet can help you identify when they started crumbling so you can begin the work of rebuilding them. Chapter 5 will help you say no when you want to and set limits with your partner.

WORKSHEET 4E

Look back into your childhood and try to remember moments when you said "No" or put your needs first. What was said to you? What happened?

_____
_____
_____
_____

If you feel unable to set limits with your partner, why do you think that is?

_____
_____
_____
_____

When you said "No" or set limits in the past with your spouse, what actually happened?

_____
_____
_____

What might you need to help you feel stronger?

_____
_____
_____

ARE YOU DOING IT ALL?

If you find taking care of your self-interests difficult, there is a good chance that it's affecting the rest of the household. When you habitually put your own needs aside in favor of your partner's or take over his responsibilities, you probably feel like a single parent with one more kid. You find yourself managing and controlling everything—and getting nothing back. One of the many problems with this arrangement is that eventually you'll burn out. Here is a picture of an ADD relationship without balance. The non-ADD spouse:

- Does all of the household tasks for the whole family, including shopping, laundry, cooking, and bill paying. She has given up asking her spouse to help.

- Makes all arrangements and keeps track of the family's social life.

- Takes it upon herself to make sure her husband gets to work and to his appointments on time.

- Makes medical or dental appointments for her spouse.

- Takes total responsibility for helping the kids with their homework, because her spouse can't focus and just gets them more confused.

- May be the only one working because her partner can't hold down a job.

Think about your relationship and whether there is give-and-take. You may be unaware of how unbalanced your relationship is, or perhaps there is more balance than you thought. The list of *Who Did What* in the next chapter will uncover the reality, as well as offer ideas about how to share the load.

NOTES TO MYSELF

CHAPTER FIVE

Working It Out

"It's never too late — in fiction or in life — to revise."

Nancy Thayer

HOW TO TALK WITH YOUR PARTNER

A husband said to his wife, "I have a joke for you. How many people with ADD does it take to screw in a light bulb?"
"I don't know," she said. "How many?"
"Do you want to go to the movies?" he replied.

As you know, communication issues in ADD relationships are unique, to say the least. It can be frustrating and unnerving to talk with someone who constantly changes the subject, is unfocused, and interrupts. I have felt stunned by what I perceived as rude and uncaring behavior from people with ADD in my life. It took me a long time before I could even say anything about it because I felt so hurt. And of course, they had no idea about what they were doing. To protect myself, I had to learn certain tricks. One was to never bring up important issues out of the blue, because they were unable to stop what they were doing to listen to me. Another was to not talk in generalities or expect them to read little cues. I had to be specific. My business partner once said, "I don't understand subtle."

Eventually, I learned to stand up for myself. Here are four ways I have expressed myself:

1. "I was talking to you and all of a sudden you started talking to the dog. I feel like you don't care about what I'm saying."

2. "Can you please stop interrupting me? I'm trying to tell you something important."

3. "I really need you to listen to me. Please put the paper down so I know you're paying attention."

4. "AAAUUUGHH!!"

To have an effective conversation, you need to do some advance planning and know how to capture your partner's attention. The most important thing to remember is that even though your spouse has ADD, you still have a right to express yourself and be heard. Here are some tips to help you talk with your partner:

- If he takes medication, make sure it's still working.

- If possible, be clear beforehand about what you want to discuss. This may mean holding onto some issues for just a little while until you can be specific.

- When talking about something important, make sure it's at a time when your spouse listens and focuses best. Is it in the early morning, when he first wakes up? Or maybe it's in the evening, after the kids are in bed?

- If you are having a planned conversation, try to anticipate any distractions or interruptions that might get him off track. Agree ahead of time not to answer the phone, and make sure the TV is off and the computer is out of sight.

- Don't try to start talking with your partner when he is involved in another activity. For example, he'll keep looking back at the computer until you are nuts with frustration. If it's important, make an appointment to talk.

- Whenever possible, be detailed in your explanations of how you felt. There are many degrees of anger. Maybe you felt annoyed instead of furious.

- If your spouse tends to interrupt frequently, work with him on creating some systems that will benefit you both. People with ADD often interrupt because they are afraid if they don't say something right then, they will forget. Suggest that he have a pen and paper handy so he can write down his thoughts until it's his turn to talk. Some couples use e-mail as part of their communication. It's an excellent way to talk without being interrupted.

- If he is antsy and can't sit still, give him something to fidget with while you're talking. I have a friend with ADD who plays games on her cell phone while we're talking. I used to feel insulted, but now I realize that she listens better that way.

- Think of an interesting way to capture your spouse for a conversation. I used to massage my husband's back and neck when I wanted him to listen. I felt better, because I knew he wouldn't go anywhere, and he was too relaxed to be distracted. (At least, when he didn't fall asleep!)

- Write down ahead of time what you'd like to discuss, so that you start the conversation off on the right foot and keep it focused. This is particularly helpful if your spouse changes directions so frequently you can't remember what your conversations were originally about. It's not uncommon to find yourself planning the family vacation when you started off talking about the food budget.

- If you perceive that your spouse's mind is wandering off, touching him (not kicking him!) will probably bring it back.

- Paraphrase and ask your spouse to do the same. Paraphrasing is a non-judgmental reflection of what the other person said and reduces misunderstandings. If you were to paraphrase, you would tell your spouse what he just said to you in your own words. And he would do the same after it was your turn to talk. If he doesn't get what you're saying, try again with different words.

- Take a problem-solving approach and turn your complaint into a request. Since it will be easy for your partner to agree to something and not follow through, help him anticipate obstacles that will get in the way. Brainstorm solutions and ask how he will be held accountable.

- Don't talk for too long. If you still have issues to get off your chest, set up another time to talk again as soon as possible.

- To protect yourself and help guarantee a better outcome, develop some ground rules for your conversations. You might want to take the initiative and present a list of rules to your mate. After you include his input, sign it and ask him to do the same. Post copies of it in your bedroom, kitchen, and other places you are inclined to talk. Here are a few suggestions to start with:

1. We assume our intentions are good and we are both doing the best we can.

2. No accusations or finger pointing, which would be irrelevant anyway if we remember #1.

3. Derogatory names or insults are not allowed.

4. Each of us gets a limited, uninterrupted time to talk.

GROUND RULES CONTRACT

I agree to abide by the following rules:

Name _____ Date _____

Name _____ Date _____

1._____
_____

2._____
_____

3._____
_____

4._____
_____

5._____
_____

6._____
_____

7._____
_____

8._____
_____

9._____
_____

10._____
_____

MAKING IT FAIR

Two ADD husbands were talking at a support group meeting. The first one said, "My wife thinks she does too much around the house. She bought me a cookbook for my birthday so I could help out."
"Did it work?" asked the other.
"Not really. I couldn't get very far because every recipe started with take a clean bowl."

Are you burned-out? Are you constantly responsible for more than your share of tasks and obligations? If so, it's time to do something about it. All happy couples have one thing in common: they share the load. It doesn't have to be a 50/50 kind of thing, but however you choose to share responsibilities should feel fair and respectful to both of you.

The first step in learning how to share responsibilities is figuring out what they are. You probably do many chores without even thinking about it. Even though you're on automatic pilot, they still take energy and time. Do you automatically fill the dog's water dish every time you walk by? The task itself isn't a big deal, but it's vitally important if you're the only one doing it.

Starting today, make a list of who did every single household and family task. Don't forget to write down everything—watering the plants, filling up the gas tank, even picking up dirty cups in the living room. Every time a task is added to the list, include how much time it took to complete it. People with ADD often have unrealistic ideas about time. They may be inclined to say, "Sure, I'll do it," thinking something will take a few seconds when it really takes a half hour. Both of you should work on the list, and it will take more than a few days to cover it all. The list of *Who Did What* on page 71 will help you start.

When you're finished with the list, identify the tasks you each don't mind, as well as those you hate. There may even be tasks you enjoy.

Some people love working in the garden and others can't stand touching dirt. I know someone who enjoys taking charge of the family accounts and paying the bills. She gets a kick out of numbers and paperwork. Her husband, on the other hand, has never balanced his checkbook.

After you've identified your likes and dislikes, start to divvy up the tasks. Think about schedules and who is best suited for each task. Take into consideration that it might be worthwhile to do more, if your partner will handle chores you hate. If you both hate the same things, you could take turns, do them together for support, or hire someone to help. Hiring help may be out of character for your family, but it's worth the expense if it gives you a break or leads to a more peaceful co-existence.

You can find hungry college kids who will work for reasonable rates. Post an ad at your local college or on a community bulletin board. Craig's List on the Web, www.craigslist.org, is also a great resource for finding help. Just click on the link to your particular city and you can access practically anything you're looking for. You can hire younger, yet responsible kids in the neighborhood who would love being a "mother's helper." Let them help with little things that make a difference in the quality of your life. How about walking the dog, folding laundry, or entertaining the kids, so one of you can make dinner? If you love the same things, enjoy them together and work as a team.

Once you've figured out future responsibilities, fill out the *Shared Chore List*. You may want to make a few copies and fill out a separate form for seasonal tasks. Write his chores in one color and yours in another so it will be easy to separate out at a glance. Since people with ADD become easily overwhelmed, make sure your spouse hasn't agreed to take on too much at once. You could suggest that he schedule one job into two or three manageable chunks of time. If his job is spring weeding, rather than planning it for one whole afternoon, he can schedule it under the *When* and *Time Period* columns for Monday, Wednesday, and Saturday, twenty minutes each time.

Although your partner may need some reminding, it's not your responsibility to make sure his tasks get done. He needs to try to develop ways to remind himself about his chores. He can find suggestions in the many books about managing ADD, or a coach can help him. A woman I know sets her phone to remind her to empty the dishwasher. You could hang out with him while he does his job to give him support and keep him on track. But only do it if you want to, and leave as soon as you start to feel restless or resentful. The two of you might want to come up with consequences and rewards. For example, if he forgets a certain percentage of his commitments, he takes you out for dinner wherever you choose. And of course, to be fair, the same deal applies to you. If you forget a certain percentage of your commitments, you have to accompany him to a movie of his choice. You can have fun creating all sorts of interesting, motivating rewards. Fill out the forms *Rewards for a Job Well Done* and *Consequences of a Job Undone.*

It will help both of you if you can find it in your heart to express appreciation when he completes his jobs. This may seem ridiculous since you're used to handling everything with little acknowledgement. Try to remember that he is different neurochemically, and what seems easy to you isn't to him. Your appreciation and respect can motivate him to keep going. Another important piece to remember is that you're also worthy of praise. If you don't get it, it's probably because he forgot, so just come out and ask for it. Get the good stuff you deserve. To reinforce this system and keep old patterns from resurfacing, set up a time for weekly meetings. Discuss how it's going and make changes as needed. To increase your chances for successful meetings, reread, *"How to Talk with Your Partner"* on page 63.

WHO DID WHAT

Chore	Who did it	Time it took

SHARED CHORE LIST

Who	What	When	Time period *(if applicable)*

REWARDS FOR A JOB WELL DONE

Name_____

If I keep_____ % of my commitments for _____(time frame)
I can choose from the following rewards:

1. _____

2. _____

3. _____

4. _____

5. _____

Name _____

If I keep _____% of my commitments for _____(time frame)
I can choose from the following rewards:

1. _____

2. _____

3. _____

4. _____

5. _____

CONSEQUENCES OF A JOB UNDONE

Name_____

If I don't keep_____ % of my commitments for _____(time frame) my partner can choose from the following consequences:

1. _____

2. _____

3. _____

4. _____

5. _____

Name_____

If I don't keep_____ % of my commitments for _____(time frame) my partner can choose from the following consequences:

1. _____

2. _____

3. _____

4. _____

5. _____

FEEDING YOUR HEART

As well as asking for what you need in the house, don't forget to ask for what you need in your heart. Expressing an emotional need may feel vulnerable, and it can set you up for rejection. But keeping your feelings inside sets you up for poor health, low self-esteem, and a compromised existence. Remember that most individuals with ADD can't take a hint. So it's very important to be open and specific.

Spend some time defining what you want and need from your partner. Be sure the ideas are coming from you, and not from your children, parents, friends, or spouse. Some of our needs can only be met from within, such as the need to feel whole, happy, or valuable. Others we can ask our partners to help us with, such as the need for intimacy, affection, understanding, and shared time. One divorced woman told me that she felt starved for appreciation in her marriage. If her husband had even once acknowledged all of her efforts and thanked her, they might still be together. Mother Teresa said, "There is more hunger for love and appreciation in this world than there is for bread."

Have a conversation with your heart, and ask what it needs and wants from your partner. Write everything down, no matter how small it seems. In matters of the heart, nothing is unimportant.

_____

_____

_____

_____

_____

_____

Find a quiet time to share these thoughts with your partner. He may want to reciprocate. Because you'll probably feel vulnerable, protect yourself by first reviewing, *"How to Talk with Your Partner"* on page 63.

TIPS TO HELP YOU SET LIMITS
OR JUST SAY NO

If you're not used to standing up for yourself when you feel taken advantage of, invaded, or badly treated by your partner, you may be shaking in your boots the first time you try. But it will get easier with practice. Taking back your personal power is crucial for your health and for the continued existence of your marriage. Here are some thoughts and tips to help you along the way:

Setting Limits:

- Realize that loving your partner does not mean taking responsibility for his life. Backing off a little (or a lot, depending on your circumstances) and letting him grow and learn can be more loving.

- Remember that setting limits helps both of you. It's a way to conserve your energy and preserve the love in your marriage.

- Spend time learning what you want and need. What is negotiable and what isn't? In order to stay strong, you need to become aware of your personal bottom line.

- Consider the fact that you can't set limits with your spouse and take care of his feelings at the same time. It's impossible.

- Find support from others who understand your struggle to remain separate and stand up for yourself. It's easy to slip back into old passive ways.

- Be aware of your tendency to take over and anticipate the needs of your partner. Make sure that he actually verbalizes a request and you aren't just assuming he wants something from you.

- Think positively about setting limits. It will get you what you want as well as protect you from what you don't want.

- Your spouse may become upset if he can't depend on you to do everything anymore. Don't feel guilty. It's OK to gradually change the rules as you learn to identify your feelings and express your needs.

- If you find setting limits impossible or unbearably stressful, you may want to talk to a therapist to help you heal and grow stronger.

Saying No:

- Give your spouse advance warning that you are going to start saying no. Explain that if you have the freedom to say no, you will feel better about saying yes. And he will never have to worry that you're agreeing to something that you don't want to do.

- If he asks you for something, remember that you have a choice. Think about whether you want to refuse or agree.

- Identify the fears or beliefs that are getting in the way of saying no. Look at them realistically to see if you're being catastrophic. Will he really go to work naked if you don't fold his clothes that have been sitting in the dryer for a week?

- If you aren't sure how you want to respond to a request, you have the right to take some time. Tell him you'll let him know at a specified later date. Be sure to give him your answer. Don't just ignore the request and hope he'll forget.

- Say no if you want, as calmly as possible.

- Explain your reasons briefly, without being defensive.

- Although it may be your tendency, remember that you don't have to ask for forgiveness or approval when saying no.

- If he persists and doesn't listen, remind him of how important it is to your relationship that you be able to say no.

HOW TO DODGE THE DARTS

Previously, we discussed the problem of our spouses aiming their frustrations at the nearest target—us. In spite of their reasons, it's important to remember that we are not a dart board for our partner's frustrations and we are not to blame for their shortcomings. If we keep our feelings inside and tolerate hurtful words or actions, we unintentionally reinforce behavior we don't want. Here are some ideas about what you can do:

- If your partner is continually sarcastic, don't tolerate it anymore. Sarcasm is cruelty in the guise of humor. Even if your spouse says, "Just kidding," the real intent of sarcasm is to cause embarrassment or dismay. And when your mate is sarcastic to you in front of others, it's a form of public humiliation. Tell him, even with your friends as witnesses, that you don't appreciate his sarcasm. In private, tell him it hurts.

- If your partner is yelling at you, try saying, "You can keep yelling if you want, but I am leaving the room. When you're ready to talk with me, I'll come back." Then leave immediately. If it happens on the phone, you don't have to listen to it. Say something like, "I'm feeling attacked and I don't like it. I'm going to hang up now and we'll talk later." Hang up before any further conversation ensues.

- Your spouse can explode at you and forget all about it an hour later. He needs to know how his behavior is affecting you. Take some time for yourself, but be clear with him that you are taking time to recover. Let him know your heart needs time to heal. He can't treat you like that without experiencing some consequences. When you come back, talk about what happened.

- If you feel uncomfortable suddenly changing your tune and refusing to tolerate behavior that went unchallenged before, you can say, "You know what? That's not OK with me anymore." He may be surprised, but you don't really have to explain or defend your new way of standing up for yourself.

- Try to stay separate emotionally from your spouse's anger. Say to yourself, "It's his anger and has nothing to do with me." It's easier said than done, but remembering that may help you be less reactive.

REHEARSING EMOTIONAL
SELF-DEFENSE

If your partner has been taking his frustrations or anger out on you, what might you do next time to stick up for yourself?

_____
_____
_____
_____
_____
_____
_____
_____
_____
_____
_____
_____

When you rehearse this scenario in your mind, how do you feel?

_____
_____
_____
_____
_____
_____
_____
_____
_____
_____

Remember that you are worthy of love and respect.

NOTES TO MYSELF

CHAPTER SIX

Survival Skills

"Don't wish me happiness—I don't expect to be happy . . . it's gotten beyond that somehow. Wish me courage and strength and a sense of humor—I will need them all."

Anne Morrow Lindbergh

FORGIVING ON A DAILY BASIS

Nobody is perfect and all of us feel annoyed at times. Our spouses with ADD, however, can try our patience and offer us frequent opportunities to become angry—even furious. That's why it's crucial to develop a forgiving climate around our relationships and a forgiving attitude inside of ourselves.

The biggest misunderstanding many of us have about forgiveness is that it means condoning what hurt us. That's not necessarily true. We may overlook or excuse what happened, but it's always a choice. Another skewed idea is that our anger protects us, and if we soften that shield, we'll get hurt again. That is also not necessarily true. We can learn from the past.

Sometimes we stay angry because we want to punish our mates or hold them accountable for their actions. When we hold onto our anger, however, we're the ones who suffer the most, because we revisit our hurt again and again. The best outcome of forgiving is that we will find peace.

Here are ten tips to promote forgiveness on a daily basis:

1. Accept the fact that you can't make your partner behave in ways you think he should. You may have a valid expectation, but there is no guarantee that your spouse will live up to it.

2. Become conscious of your rules for others. Let go of unrealistic demands.

3. To reduce the possibility of frustration or disappointment, try to think of multiple ways to get what you want. Let's say you hate the idea of cooking and want to eat at a restaurant tonight. Before you bring it up to your husband, create contingency plans that will feel OK if he doesn't want to go. Some possibilities are

that he cooks, you order out, or you invite a friend to go out for dinner instead.

4. Maintain a private space so when you feel anger coming on you can take a "time-out" as soon as possible to process your feelings. You are entitled to as much time as you need to reflect upon what is upsetting you.

5. Do your best every day to let go of anger and resentment. Realize the act of forgiving is for your benefit—it will make your heart lighter.

6. Don't deny negative feelings, but try to cultivate gratitude and an awareness of the positive. If your mate did something wrong, remember all the times he did something right.

7. As soon as you feel upset, practice a stress-reduction technique such as exercising, calling a friend, or taking some slow, deep breaths.

8. Try to see the other side of the story. You may be sure you're right until you put yourself in your partner's shoes.

9. Become clear about what is upsetting you and talk to your mate about it. Don't let your feelings fester for too long.

10. Figure out what you need in order to forgive. Would it help if he apologized? Agreed to hire a coach? Baked you a dozen cookies?

LOVING DETACHMENT

Wayland Myers, Ph.D., has generously contributed this article. Although the practice of loving detachment is beneficial for all relationships, it is especially significant for the readers of this book.

Many years ago, I heard a counselor say, "Loving detachment is a means whereby we allow others the opportunity to learn how to care for themselves better." At the time, I was struggling painfully with my child's drug and alcohol use. Those words both confused and disturbed me. Did they mean I should abstain from trying to control my child's addictive behaviors? That I should not try to protect her? It sounded like some form of self-protective abandonment.

But over time, I came to see the counselor's point. I slowly discovered a number of benefits to using loving detachment as a way of relating to anyone struggling with self-harming behaviors. I also came to see that it applied to any person whose successful life management required them to practice good self-care over long periods of time. With these expanded visions, I became excited about how many situations and relationships would benefit from the practice of loving detachment.

Let me start by giving you my current definition. I consider myself lovingly detached when:

I am willing and able to compassionately, and without judgment, allow others to be different from me, to be self-directed, and to be responsible for taking care of themselves.

Here are four ways that I believe detachment is loving for those I love, and four ways I consider it loving for me.

How Detachment is Loving for Others:

1. *Those I care for might learn to look within, and trust themselves for self-direction, including when and how to ask for help.*

If I refrain from trying to manage their problematic situation, the people I care about may learn something about thinking for themselves, problem solving, and when and how to ask for help. They might learn to better listen to their feelings and intuitions, to heed those little voices we all wish we listened to more. They might learn to better recognize when they want help and how to request it in ways that leave them feeling good, rather than embarrassed or ashamed. In short, letting them manage their own affairs gives them the opportunity to draw on their own inner resources, instead of mine, and from this direct experience of their abilities, no matter how groping or uncertain, they can build competence and may thereby increase their confidence. I believe this is the number one, and most natural, avenue for creating an increased sense of self-esteem.

2. *They might learn more about cause and effect.*

My decision not to intervene allows others to have an uninterrupted experience of the cause-and-effect relationship between their actions and the natural consequences of those actions. In this way, they have a direct encounter with their personal power to contribute to their own pleasure or pain. Allowing people to have appropriately sized, real problems, and real responsibility for working out their solutions, seems to greatly facilitate this learning.

3. *They might experience the motivation to continue on, or change.*

Pleasurable and painful experiences often provide us the motivation to repeat what brought satisfaction and change what didn't. We all use this kind of emotional energy to move us forward in life. These motivating energies arise naturally within us and feel much better to respond to than the attempts by others to motivate us through guilt, fear, and other forms of coercion.

4. *Self-discovery and self-enjoyment might increase.*

If I grant others the freedom to think, feel, value, perceive, etc. as they wish, and they relax because they feel respected and safe, they might discover many new things about themselves. They might discover what they really like, feel, or think. They might have moments of creative insight that inspire, excite, and encourage them. They might invent new, more satisfying dreams for their lives than ever would have appeared under the pressure of my controlling presence. Whenever I find myself struggling with the impulse to step in and begin trying to manage another's life, or solve his or her problems, I find it helpful to review the four points just presented. They strongly motivate me to remain lovingly detached.

How Detachment is Loving for Me:

1. *I am relieved of the strain of attempting the impossible.*

By carefully reviewing my experiences of trying to control other people's physical behaviors, sobriety, health, learning, emotions and opinions, I have come to one conclusion: The only thing I might be able to control is a person's physical behavior—and that requires that I possess enough physical strength and am willing to use it. If I accept my powerlessness to control the other things—the inner lives and wills of others—then I relieve myself of the stress and strain of attempting the impossible. This is a primary way for me to create more serenity in my life. In fact, if I practice this process deeply enough, I sometimes reach the point where I form no opinion about what another should do. This is a truly liberated and refreshing moment for us both.

2. *What other people think of me can become none of my business.*

If I am powerless to control the thoughts, perceptions, values, or emotions of another, then I can liberate myself by accepting that their opinions of me are none of my business. Accepting this as fact, I not only free myself, but the other person as well, because I cease my attempts to control their inner workings.

3. *My attention and energy are freed to focus on improving my own life.*

I have plenty of problem areas in my own life. Obsessing about another's life can help me avoid the pain within mine. But the time and energy I spend obsessing about another's life is time and energy that I don't spend on mine, and if I do this enough, my life stays at its current level of unmanageability—or gets worse. Loving detachment gives me the opportunity to invest my energies in my own life.

4. *I can express my love or caring in ways that bring me joy and satisfaction.*

When someone I care for is struggling with a problem, or feeling some kind of pain, I usually want to be supportive or helpful. But I want to offer the kind of help that would bring me joy to offer, and them joy to receive. One of the ways that I have developed a picture of what this help could look like is to recall the times when caring friends or others have offered me assistance in ways that I enjoyed. What did they do? While showing no sign that they felt responsible for solving my problems, they offered me four things:

- *Their compassionate, empathic understanding of how I perceived and felt about my situation.*

- *Their experiences and learning from similar situations for my consideration.*

- *Their genuine optimism about my abilities to work through my struggles.*

- *Their willingness to help, on my terms, in ways that were congruent with their needs.*

To be offered understanding, companionship, encouragement, and assistance, but not interference, is the most satisfying help I have known. Offering this to others increases both the joy in my life and my own self-esteem. Looking at the eight ways that I see detachment as being loving, I conclude that the most basic reason for practicing it is to provide an opportunity for both people's lives to be improved. The lives of those I love may be improved because I respect their powers of self-care enough to let them have a chance to reap the potential benefits of struggling, learning, and succeeding on their own. My life is improved because I avoid unnecessary distress, retain energy I might have wasted, and offer caring and support in ways that bring me joy. In these ways, loving detachment plays a powerful and rewarding role in helping me to both live, and let live.

When to Help . . . When to Lovingly Detach:

OK, loving detachment is great for everyone, but how do I decide when to do it? I lovingly detach when I conclude that it is the *most helpful* action I can take. There are times when I believe that actually helping out is probably the most helpful thing. Then I go ahead and help. But there are other times when I conclude that detaching with love is probably the stronger, deeper form of love; the deeper gift. How do I figure this out? I ask myself questions like these:

1. Which action, helping or lovingly detaching, do I believe will strengthen my loved one the most *in the long run*? This is my primary question.

2. Does the "help" I am thinking of providing involve me picking up a responsibility which would normally be theirs,

but which they are not performing at the levels I believe would be best? Am I remembering for them, organizing for them, planning ahead for them, making peace for them, apologizing for them, keeping track of something for them, anticipating consequences for them? It has been my frequent experience that as long as I continue to handle jobs like these for my loved ones, their level of job performance rarely improves, and they often resent my interventions. But, I don't let myself complain too much because, after all, I *am* a volunteer.

3. Is the crisis I am tempted to help them with one that is a *natural* consequence of their choices or behaviors? Generally, I prefer to let people encounter the full force of the natural consequences of their actions because I want to allow them the maximum opportunity to learn and become motivated to change. However, I make exceptions to this preference if I believe the emotional or physical harm involved will be at a level *I cannot live with* in the long run. When in doubt, I always choose the action options I believe *I* can live with best in the long run.

4. Will the intervention I am considering create a crisis which is not in the natural order of things? If I express my hurt or disappointment concerning how they have treated me, and that creates a crisis between us that might be in the natural order of life, something that is natural to occur. However, if I consistently nag and pressure them, that might create a crisis that I would *not* label as natural because my choosing to nag is just *an* option in life, not a necessity.

5. If I think my loved one would benefit by encountering consequences for one of their actions, are there any naturally occurring ones available that I can let do the job? I'd rather have my loved one hate the consequences, than hate me for creating them.

6. Are any of the helpful things I've gotten into the habit of doing for them things which it might be better for them to

learn to do for themselves? Are there any jobs I'd like to retire from that would be in the natural order of life for them to learn how to do for themselves? If so, I invite myself to retire.

I hope all of these thoughts and suggestions help you figure out when, how, and how much to help those you love, and to be more at ease when you chose to lovingly abstain. I have not found loving detachment to be a painless activity. I usually suffer, but my suffering is lessened because I believe that, by resisting my urge to help, I am offering the person I love the highest form of love I can. I wish you well.

Wayland Myers is a psychologist and consultant living in the north coastal region of San Diego County, California. He specializes in working with the family side of the addictive process, post traumatic stress reduction using EMDR, communication training, and improving the quality of marital relationships.

I CAN'T STAND IT ANYMORE

Unfortunately, the title of this page describes a frustration that is real for too many. You can learn as much as possible, try a myriad of approaches, and support your partner, but sometimes circumstances just don't get better. If this is your situation, here are more ideas that might help:

- Figure out when your partner last saw his prescribing professional. If it's been awhile, he may need his medication adusted or changed.

- Is he skipping doses or taking his meds whenever he feels like it? You can't follow him around and hand out his pills, but you can talk to him about taking his meds on the prescribed schedule. The nature of ADD means difficulty remembering things, including medications. Ask if he wants you to remind him, but be sure to ask before you automatically take this on. You'll end up even more frustrated if all the effort is coming from you. If he wants your help, buy him a seven-day pill box, divided into morning, afternoon, and evening time periods. Or create a medication log for him to fill out. It might even be worthwhile to develop a reward system together. Figure out how to keep track, and create a motivating reward for when he takes his medicine consistently for a predetermined period of time. A sexy night at a hotel?

- Maybe you're pointing your finger at ADD and it's more than that. Does he drink too much? Is he depressed? Take it upon yourself to make doubly sure his diagnostician is qualified to rule out and treat comorbid conditions.

- If he's tried a number of traditional medications that haven't worked, it could be time for another approach. Ask if he wants your help in finding a good homeopathic or naturopathic physican, specializing in ADD.

- Bring in a third party for support, such as a coach or counselor. It will be a tremendous relief to have the burden lifted from you. Objective, quality help from outside the marriage can feel like divine intervenion.

- As mentioned in chapter 3, seek the help of a marriage counselor if the relationship is full of hurt and resentment. Couple's counseling can help both of you heal, renew your love, and re-establish trust. Choose a professional who understands how ADD impacts a relationship.

- Buy some books about managing the symptoms of ADD and read them together. Make some popcorn, cuddle (if your frustration will allow that), and take turns reading out loud.

- Wach a videotape about ADD together. Two places to find them are the ADD Resources lending library, (www.addresources.org) and Mindworks Press, (www.amenclinics.com).

- Attend ADD support and information groups together. Be strong in your assertion that he accompany you.

- Keep reminding yourself that he has a brain disorder.

- If he is really trying to grow and improve the relationship, dig deep for patience. Changing lifelong habits takes a lot of time and repetition.

- Pay less attention to your spouse and more attention to you. Take part in activities or events that bring you joy and healing.

- Find a therapist for yourself. You deserve someone who will truly listen to your concerns, especially if your spouse can't.

- Identify two or three behaviors that are intolerable and make you feel the worst. Work with your spouse to improve just those things, instead of everything at once.

- If the clutter and messiness are driving you up a wall, lower your standards. You've probably already done that out of necessity, but making it a conscious decision can lessen some of the stress.

- Expand your knowledge and personal exploration of boundaries. Read books such as *Facing Codependence* by Pia Mellody and join a codependency support group.

- Make a conscious attempt to remember why you love him. Plan a night out at least once a month, with the goal of enjoying yourselves and not talking about problems.

- If possible, figure out ways to cope with difficult behaviors without trying to change them. If he is always late getting out the door, take two cars and go ahead by yourself. If you're burned-out and he's too distracted to effectively help your children with homework, hire a high school student to help.

- Get support from other non-ADD spouses on an online forum. Some forums even include a private section that is like a shelter where nobody can find you. Visit www.addforums.com and give and get support from others who are struggling with the same issues.

- Develop an awareness of what you are telling yourself on a daily basis. Our inner voices have a huge influence over how we think and feel. You may be shocked to discover you're giving yourself messages such as "I'm so stupid," "I can't take this anymore," or "I'm going to die if I have to live this way much longer." Make a note about what you are telling yourself as soon as you realize it. Once you become aware of those kinds of thoughts, please find help and support. If that kind of harmful self-talk remains unconscious, it can make you miserable, ill, or corrode your insides like acid.

- If you're doing all the work to hold your marriage together, it may be time to re-evaluate. Does your partner refuse to accept help or even try to change? Has the stress and frustration in your relationship affected your health? If so, tell your partner you're at the end of your rope. Don't hold back about how unhappy you are. Maybe it will motivate him to get help. There is only so much one person can do. You deserve a partner who truly cares about your needs and feelings.

DO SOMETHING NOW!

If you are feeling at your wit's end, what can you do to initiate positive change in your relationship and/or within yourself?

_____
_____
_____
_____
_____
_____
_____
_____
_____
_____
_____
_____
_____
_____
_____
_____
_____
_____
_____
_____
_____
_____
_____
_____
_____
_____
_____
_____
_____

NOTES TO MYSELF

_____
_____
_____
_____
_____
_____
_____
_____
_____
_____
_____
_____
_____
_____
_____
_____
_____
_____
_____
_____
_____
_____
_____
_____
_____
_____
_____
_____
_____
_____
_____
_____
_____
_____
_____

CHAPTER SEVEN

Thriving

*"I celebrate myself,
and sing myself."*

Walt Whitman

THE IMPORTANCE OF
YOUR OWN SPACE

A side effect of a busy life is a messy home, and most of us have other priorities besides cleaning. When your spouse has ADD, however, the mess can get out of control. The clutter replicates itself a minute after it disappears, and the chaos will find its way into your being. That is why it's so vital that non-ADD partners have a space of their own—to create an environment conducive for relaxation and healing.

I practice a moving meditation called "qigong" in a particular room in my house. Whenever I enter the room, I feel calm. It is relatively free of clutter, and decorated with candles, plants, and books. When I let them, my daughters like to do their homework in that room. They say it "just feels good" in there. Maybe it's the "chi" or healing energy that they perceive. You can create such a place in your own house—whether it's in the basement, a corner surrounded by a screen, or an extra room.

Once you have found your space, you should have complete freedom to make it your own. Paint it orange if you want. Furnish it or decorate it with whatever feels good, which means anything from a shrine, to a comfortable reading chair, to a VCR for watching movies of your choice. No one can say, "How can you watch that junk?" You have the right to do whatever you want here. Have fun bringing in objects that symbolize calmness or pleasure and create your own shelter from the storm.

WARNING: DO NOT ENTER!

If you had a space of your own, what would it look like?

_____
_____
_____
_____
_____
_____
_____

How would you keep it private?

_____
_____
_____
_____
_____
_____
_____
_____

What would you do there?

_____
_____
_____
_____
_____
_____
_____
_____

DEVELOPING STRESS MUSCLES

All of our lives involve stress, but non-ADD spouses face more than their share. The stress occurs because our partners greatly impact our lives, but we feel unable to control or manage the situation. It also happens when we feel angry, frustrated, or scared with no respite or resolution in sight. Regardless of whether or not our circumstances will change, we must become proactive in taking care of ourselves. When we find ways to bring joy and calm into our lives in spite of the stressors, we move beyond surviving into thriving.

We can begin to get proactive by measuring our "stress muscles." In other words, how strong are we in our ability to ward off the negative effects of tension? If we practice certain beliefs and activities on a daily basis, we will be better able to cope. To measure your stress muscles, mark the appropriate letter in front of each of these statements:

O = often
S = sometimes
N = never

____ I have at least two friends with whom I talk often.
____ I make sure I do something calming after a stressful experience.
____ I have hobbies or interests just for me.
____ I exercise at least three times a week.
____ I have a spiritual practice, whether it is worship, meditation, or
       walking in the woods.
____ I laugh as often as possible.
____ I read or watch something uplifting at least once a week.
____ I take quiet time for myself every day.
____ I recognize tension in my body and know ways to reduce it.
____ I am aware of my breathing and periodically take a deep breath.
____ I eat a balanced meal at least once a day.
____ I am aware of and limit the alcohol I drink.
____ I am aware of and limit the sugar I eat.

___I am aware of and limit the caffeine I drink.
___I express my feelings to the important people in my life.
___I am able to receive and give affection.
___I practice accepting what I cannot change.
___I have control over my finances.
___I can say no.
___I make a conscious effort to reward myself.
___I know where to find help when I need it.

How many O's, S's and N's did you mark? If there are more than five "nevers," you need to make a few changes in order to build up those stress muscles.

What other beliefs and activities would help you manage stress?

_____
_____
_____
_____
_____
_____
_____
_____

What is the single most helpful thing you could do every day?

_____
_____
_____
_____
_____
_____
_____
_____

OUR BODIES TENSED AND RELAXED

When we are feeling stressed, our endocrine system responds by releasing hormones that are meant to help us survive in dangerous situations. Those hormones cause digestion to stop, blood sugar levels to rise, and the heart to pump more blood into the muscles. This response is supposed to help us in a short-term emergency, not on a daily basis. If our stress is unrelenting, we may experience more colds and viruses, digestive problems such as diarrhea, heartburn or constipation, skin conditions, etc. Some people believe stress contributes to very serious illnesses such as heart disease, strokes, cancer, and autoimmune diseases.

Before you get too alarmed about what might happen to you, let's look at how relaxation can heal these responses to stress. When we relax:

- Our central nervous system is taken out of the arousal state.

- Blood to the heart and skeletal muscles decreases, and flow is restored to other organs.

- Muscle tension is reduced.

- Blood pressure and heart rate are lowered.

- There is a decreased output of fight-or-flight hormones.

- Perspiration is reduced.

- Our breathing slows down and deepens.

- Digestion is more effective.

- Our immune systems are strengthened and modulated.

- We sleep better.

A PERSONAL DEFINITION
OF RELAXATION

Relaxation means different things to different people. Some possibilities are slow, easy breaths; a feeling of peace; and a clear, focused mind.

Can you recall a time when you felt calm and relaxed? Describe the situation.

_____
_____
_____
_____
_____
_____
_____
_____
_____
_____

When you think of being relaxed, what does it look and feel like?

_____
_____
_____
_____
_____
_____
_____
_____
_____
_____

MEDITATION AND GUIDED IMAGERY

Meditating can help you relax and reduce the negative effects of stress. If you've never meditated before, it's worth a try. And you'll be in good company. Famous people such as Albert Einstein and Thomas Edison supposedly practiced various forms of meditation.

Many people, however, have difficulty stilling their minds enough to experience the benefits of meditation—especially if they are required to just concentrate on their breathing or repeat a word or syllable. If you're one of those people, using guided imagery can be much more enjoyable. Guided imagery uses the imagination to take us to calming, healing places.

Imagery is the method the mind uses to communicate with the body. Our mind processes most of what we do through images, rather than words. When we remember events or experiences, we usually think of them with sounds, feelings, pictures, tastes, and sensations. Think, for example, of drinking cold lemonade on a hot day. Rather than thinking of it in words, you most likely hear the welcome crunch of ice between your teeth, taste the flavor, see the glass, feel the cold condensation under your fingers, and feel the warmth of the sun on your shoulders. Your body may have reacted in some way to what your mind imagined. Maybe you shivered or began to salivate. When we imagine calming, peaceful scenarios, our bodies react in a positive way.

Many of us are so used to feeling tense that it's become our natural state. It takes practice to learn how to physically relax or even recognize how it feels. And the more we practice, the more quickly we'll be able to release our tension—a very good skill for those living with ADD. On the next page is a script for a guided imagery exercise about a special place, designed to bring you into a state of peace and contentment. There are three ways to use it:

1. If you have a good memory, read it a few times until you get the general idea. Then close the book and begin. When you finish,

reread the script to see if there was anything you forgot for next time.

2. Record your voice reading the script and play it for yourself when you want to relax. Be sure to read it in a very slow and soothing voice, so your mind will have time to grasp the instructions and images. Give yourself at least three minutes in your special place with silence or occasional reminders to relax.

4. Ask someone you trust to read it to you, or take turns reading it to each other.

However you choose to practice this exercise, be sure to continue lying down or sitting quietly for a few minutes after you open your eyes. This is because occasionally people experience a little dizziness if they get up too abruptly after a relaxation exercise. Besides, you deserve as much time as possible before you come back to reality. If there is anything in the script that bothers you or doesn't feel natural, substitute your own ideas and words. This can be just a beginning.

IMPORTANT:

Relaxation from this exercise can cause a dreamy state, so please don't listen to a recording of it while driving.

MY SPECIAL PLACE

This meditation was created to help you let go of tension and any events that have caused you stress or discomfort. It will begin by helping you relax completely and comfortably, then it will engage your imagination, and finally it will bring you back into this place—relaxed and alert.

Whether you are sitting up or lying down, make yourself as comfortable as possible . . . with your arms relaxed and your legs uncrossed. Whenever you are ready to focus within, close your eyes and take some slow, cleansing breaths. Allow yourself to relax with each breath, letting go of any problems or worries. Remember that this is a time just for you, so you can unwind and let go. Allow any unwanted thoughts to just drift away, as easily as they came. With every exhalation, you will relax more and more. Feel your whole body becoming limp and heavy, sinking into the chair or bed that is supporting you . . . and notice how relaxed you have become, from the top of your head to the tips of your toes. Feel a wave of relaxation spread down from your head, to your neck and shoulders, all the way down your arms to your hands, to your fingertips . . . then down your spine to your legs, your feet, and your toes.

Know that although you are relaxed, you will be able to come to full alertness any time if needed, so you can let yourself go and feel peace and well-being. In a few moments, imagine that you are visiting a beautiful place, a special place that brings you feelings of comfort. Maybe you have already been there, maybe you would like to go there, maybe it is just in your imagination. Envision the scene as if you are there right now. What do you see? What do you hear? Feel the air; is it warm and humid . . . or cool and refreshing? Can you feel any breezes? Notice any colors or textures, smells, and tastes. Take your time and fully enjoy being in this beautiful place. Relax. You deserve this time just for you. You are calm, safe, and content in this place of your choosing.

Now take a few deep breaths once more and slowly begin to come back to this room . . . start to feel your fingers and toes. Slowly and gently move them; you can even wiggle them a little if you want. Take a few more minutes and then gently stretch your body . . . now open your eyes and look around. You are relaxed in this place, refreshed, alert, and awake. All is well.

AFFIRMATIONS FOR
NON-ADD SPOUSES

You may think affirmations are silly. Maybe they remind you of New-Age thinking, or the overused and familiar statement, "Every day, in every way, I am getting better and better." But specific and well-stated affirmations are genuinely helpful. They can reduce negative thinking and have been proven, if used consistently, to bring about desired changes in our health and well-being. Some people listen to recorded affirmations, others say them out loud, and still others write them on three-by-five-inch index cards placed where they will see them every day.

The following affirmations have been created to address the particular challenges of non-ADD partners. As in the preceding meditation, only utilize what feels comfortable to you and feel free to change any of it. Perhaps these statements will inspire you to create other affirmations that are more applicable to your particular situation. Try some out for a few weeks and observe any differences in how you feel. Throughout the day, you may find yourself remembering the affirmations that are meaningful.

AFFIRMATIONS

- I no longer need to be tense. I can relax and let go.

- I know that whatever I am feeling each moment is valid and true.

- I can release unwanted emotions once they have been acknowledged, and regain my inner peace.

- Every day I am more able to let go of unrealistic demands and expectations for _____ (spouse)

- I can accept my feelings without blame or criticism.

- More and more I am able to forgive _____ (spouse) for his/her limitations and mistakes of the past.

- More and more I am able to forgive myself for my limitations and mistakes of the past.

- I let go of worrying about things I cannot control and focus on my own sense of peace.

- Every day I remember that ADD is a disorder and is nobody's fault.

- I am getting better and better at standing up for myself.

- Letting go of responsibility for _____ (spouse) is not the same as abandonment. I let go in love, without guilt.

- I can soften my anger and resentment for the sake of my own well-being.

- Each day I get better at protecting and caring for myself.

- I spend my energy on what is most important to me.

- More and more, I am able to recognize my limits and ask for whatever help or guidance I need.

- I have the right to remove myself from situations that are disturbing or harmful to me.

- Every day, I feel more balance and peace in my life.

- I deserve to love and be loved.

A DATE WITH YOURSELF

Although you no doubt enjoy your partner's company, it's vital for your well-being that you regularly take time away to recharge your batteries. The energy of someone with ADD can be exciting—and draining. You deserve time for yourself outside of work and family responsibilities. After a weekend, a day, or even an hour on your own, you'll return with more patience and objectivity. There are lots of possibilities for an enjoyable time away: hiking in the woods, going to the movies, coffee with a friend, even lunch alone with a good book.

Plan a time just for yourself. What will you do?

_____

When will you do it?

_____
_____
_____

If you can't take time for yourself, why is that?

_____

What arrangements have to be made to allow time for you? What beliefs have to be changed?

_____
_____
_____

BRIEF ACTIONS TO FIND
SLIVERS OF PEACE

Although all of us would like to get away, meditate, or spend relaxing time in our own space, it isn't always possible. So here are some quick ways to grab some peace and feel a little better—in spite of the chaos around you.

- Breathe. Most of us take rapid, shallow breaths when we're stressed. Stop what you are doing every once in a while to become aware of your breathing. Breathing increases oxygen in the blood, which makes us feel calmer, less fatigued, and more alert.

- Take a "time-out," even if you have to hide in a closet to do so. During your time-out, you can say a prayer, repeat a healing affirmation, or eat some chocolate.

- If you feel emotionally knocked off your feet, do a quick exercise to help you find your center. Stand with your legs shoulder width apart, your knees unlocked, and your whole body relaxed. Close your eyes and take a few natural, calming breaths. Feel the ground beneath your feet. Imagine your feet sinking down, deep within the earth, like the roots of a strong, healthy tree. Imagine your head reaching up to the pure blue sky. Stay like this for a minute a two, knowing you are like that tree—strong, swaying, and unbreakable.

- Let yourself cry. When your mate has ADD, frustration and hurt can build up. We hold in our tears for both important and trivial reasons. Unless someone is depressed or using tears as manipulation, crying is usually healthy. It releases our tension and can lessen our pain. After a good cry, we usually feel better.

- Take a warm shower. Let the water rain down on top of your head, massaging your scalp and relaxing your shoulders. Or light a candle, play some music, and luxuriate in a soothing bath.

- Communicate. Whenever possible, talk with your mate about what is bothering you. Holding it in will create more stress for you. He may forget all about an upsetting incident, but you won't. Why shoulder that all by yourself?

- If you are going nuts at home, grab the phone and call a friend. Share your feelings and get support, or become involved in your friend's life for awhile. That small connection with someone outside of your family can give you new energy and perspective.

- Walk around the block. Try to let go of what is worrying you and pay attention to the beauty in your surroundings; really look at the autumn leaves, summer flowers, architecture, or the faces of people passing by.

- Pat yourself on the back for what you accomplish every day, for all you put up with, and for what a strong, loving person you are. Give yourself a reward. You deserve it.

NOTES TO MYSELF

YOU YOURSELF, AS MUCH AS ANYBODY IN THE ENTIRE UNIVERSE, DESERVE YOUR LOVE AND AFFECTION.

BUDDHA